Sky Writing

By the same author:

Poetry

Hunger Games

Life Sentences

The June Fireworks

High Wire

Dark Cupboards New Rooms

This Cathedral Grief

The Dancing Man

Fiction

The Blessing

A Winter Sowing

Casualties of Love

Narrative non-fiction

The White: Last Days in the Antarctic Expeditions
of Scott and Mawson 1911-1913

Literary and Cultural Criticism

Dividing Lines: Poetry, Class and Ideology in the 1930s

Taking it Like a Man: Suffering, Sexuality and the War Poets

Kenneth Slessor

Sky Writing

ADRIAN CAESAR

WITH

Artworks by Kat Rae

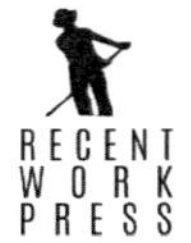

Sky Writing
Recent Work Press
Canberra, Australia

ISBN: 9781764106849

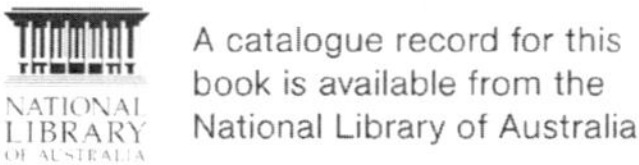

A catalogue record for this book is available from the National Library of Australia

Cover and layout design:
Soile Paloheimo, Palo Design Ltd

recentworkpress.com

For my Granddaughters

Charlie and Olivia

and in memory of

K. and R.

Contents

Prologue:

My sister, when she knew she was dying,
bequeathed two rings to my granddaughters.
They were given to her by her first lover.
'*You can tell your girls the story*,' she said.

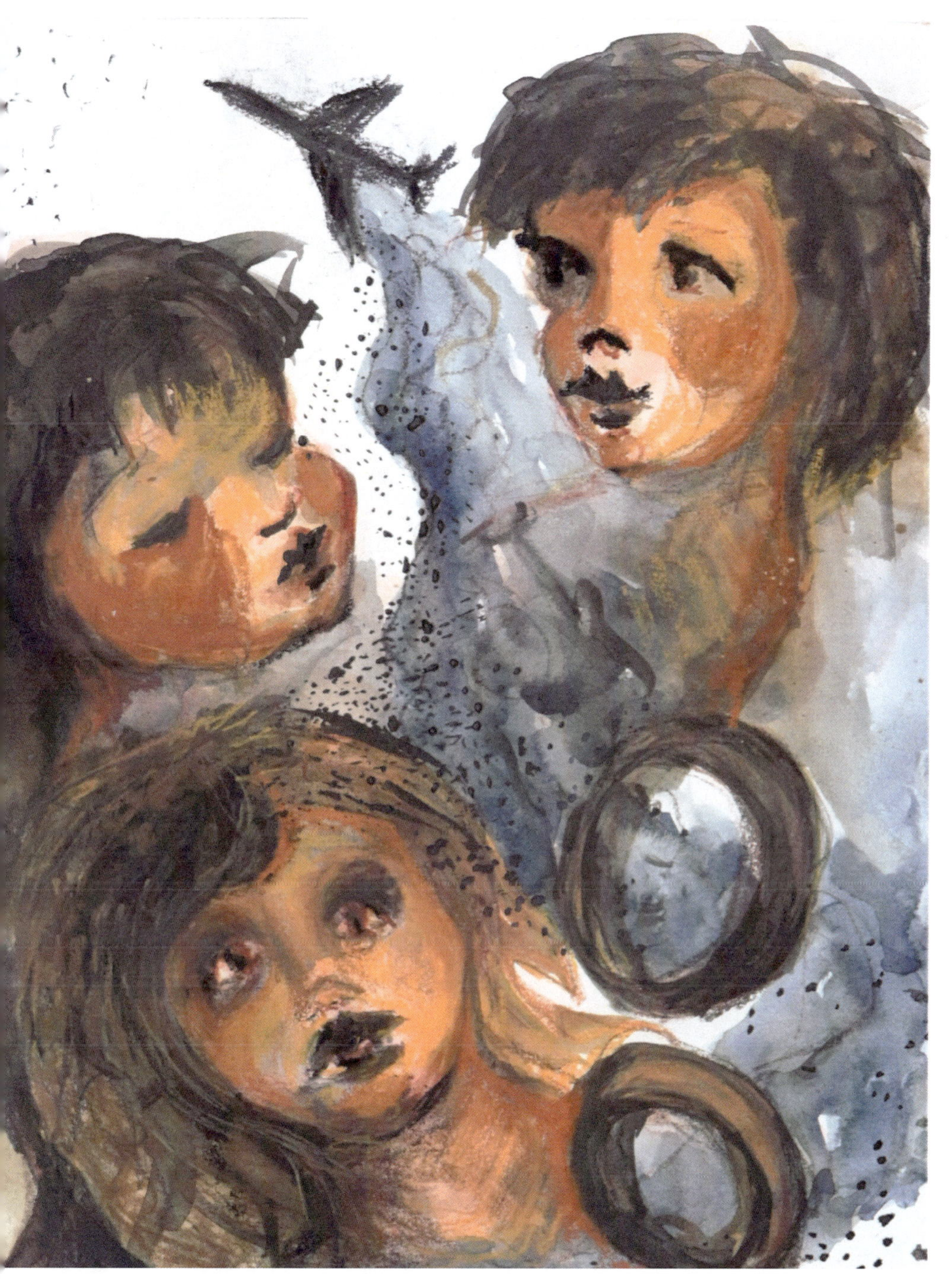

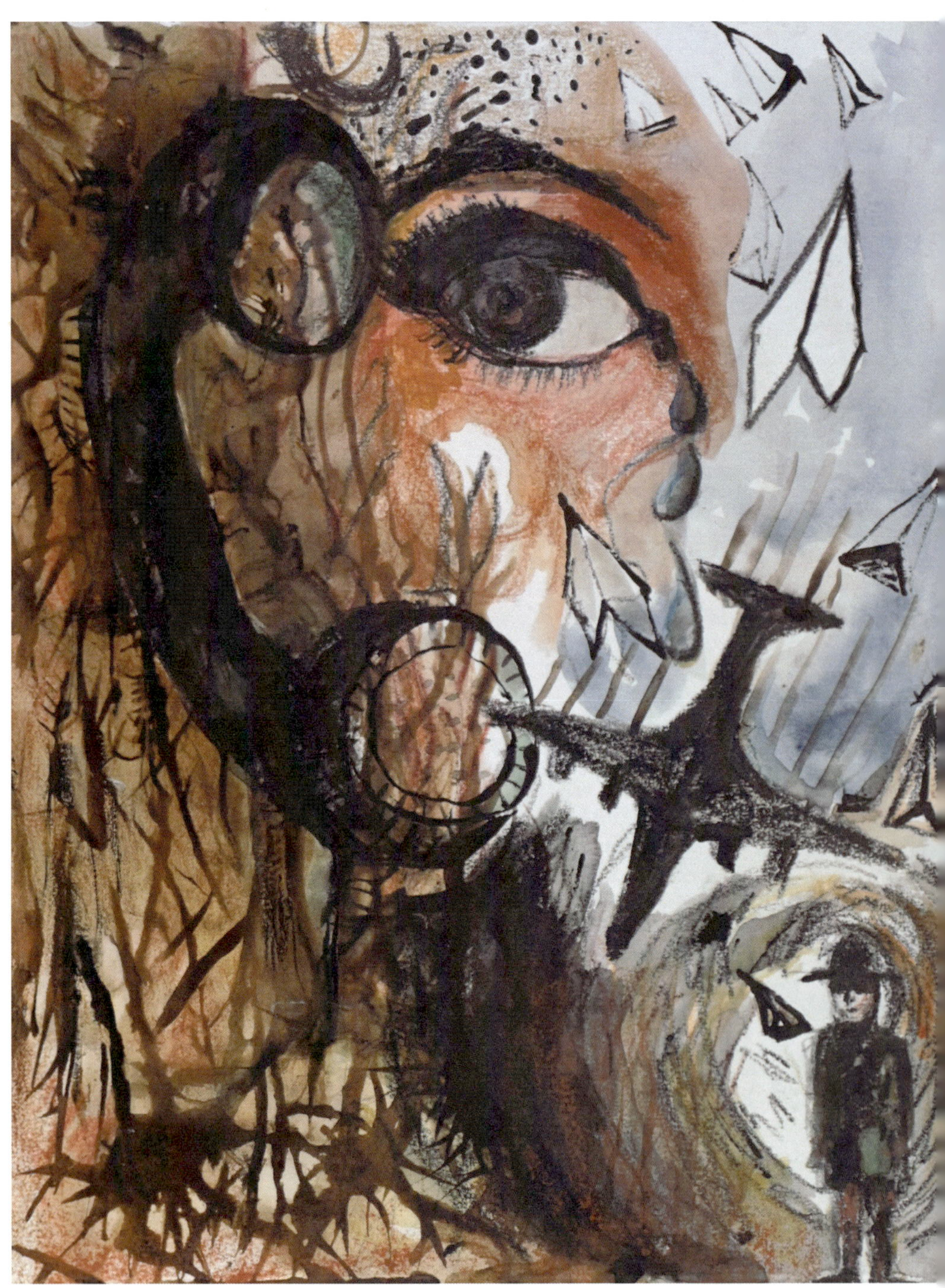

Sister: A Letter

You will have had the news.
        I couldn't tell you
though you will understand
        there is no one else for me
to talk to   so this wrench
        and   stretch   of words
to wire   defying   ghostly
        dis   connections.

Since I heard I can't bear
        the telephone
not that speech frightens me
        so much as the violent silence
                                that follows
as if every conversation might end
        with such abrupt   ironic
                                termination.

Cut   off

I don't know how

to reach you   to mourn

        through this unhappy medium

all the lines
                        break
                                                down

        to this   arid   repetition

He is dead.   He is
                                Not.

Brother: Report

An air-force pilot
died yesterday
while practising
low-level
aerobatics.

No other aircraft
were involved.

It is thought
he attempted
to eject
too late   and was killed
instantly.

A coronial enquiry and
Air-crash investigation
will proceed in due course.

So, in brief
it was reported
and a joust begins
between *pilot error*
and *mechanical failure*

while I begin this in
quest
a morbid carnival
of words
twisting
diving
looping
to trace   an imaginary
meaning

or provisional   unfinding

as he inscribed   the sky

with disappearing   vapour

trails.

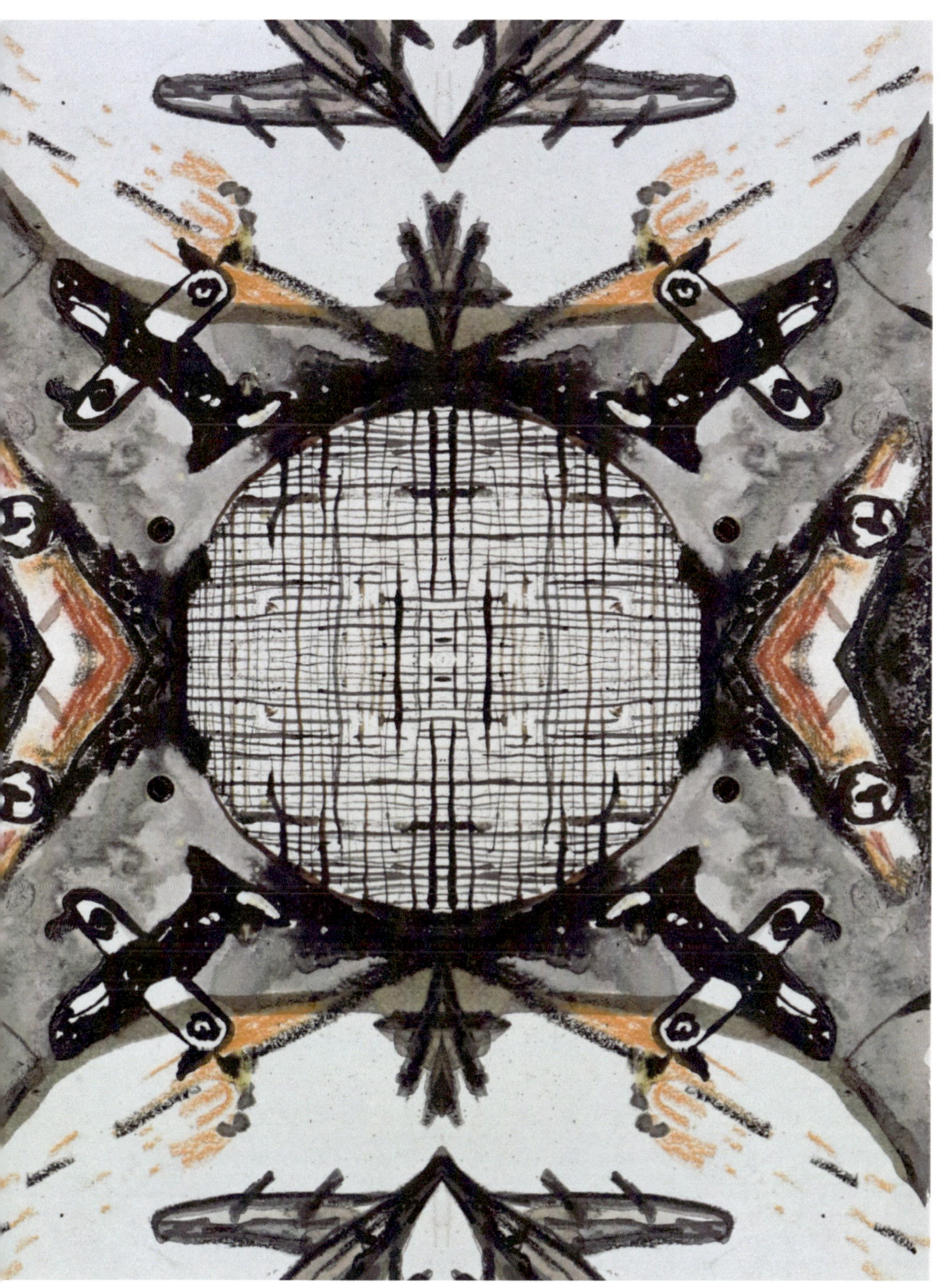

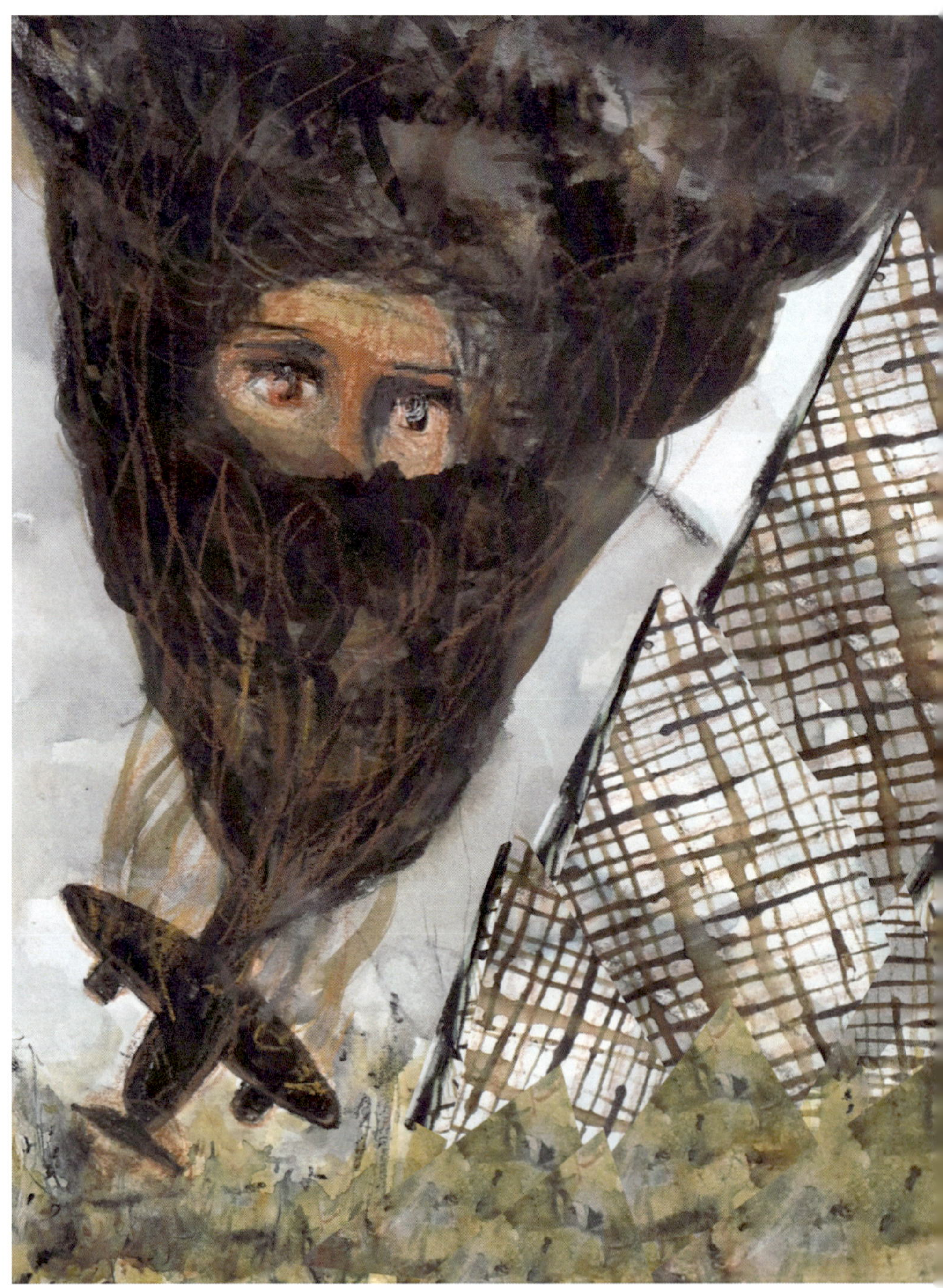

Sister: Premonition

Did I tell you
        the night before he died
in dream I saw it all

a flash of silver
        against black
the plane spiralling to
        lurid explosion?

I know it's common
                        to dream
of flight   and falling
        this cruel
        coincidence evokes

my early inhibitions
        in the act of love.

He flew for thrills
        I was always afraid

of   flying.

Brother: Preparations

I have the photograph. We are all there
boy-scouts at the Christmas Fete,
teenagers clustered round an unlikely
Santa Claus, our gangling arms
badged with what we thought
were all the arts and crafts of survival.

Yet two didn't make it
to thirty. One learnt knots too well,
entangled in some late afternoon
hotel he hangs, a lawyer for whom
the law was not enough.

The other, your lover,
erased himself in a fast moment
under an illusion of control
false as charity.

Prepared for nothing
not prepared, all that's left
are the smiles of innocence,

each grim rictus a lifeless print
that leads to this funereal art,
attempting to map the past,
scouting a future.

Brother: Lost Chances

Remember the game, parents absent,
after fish and chips, clandestine beer,

spinning bottles in the dark to win a kiss
how carefully a twisting wrist

could from the circle of friends
elicit the desired desiring lips,

salt and vinegar on the tongue
a piquant taste of later tears.

Did love for him become
the proffered acid sponge

which made him play another game
controlling spin the plane

then spearing life for pure experience
from which there is no resurrection,

leaving my sister, weeping Magdalene,
rotating the bottle empty in the room

pervaded by absence she recalls
but cannot give kisses of life.

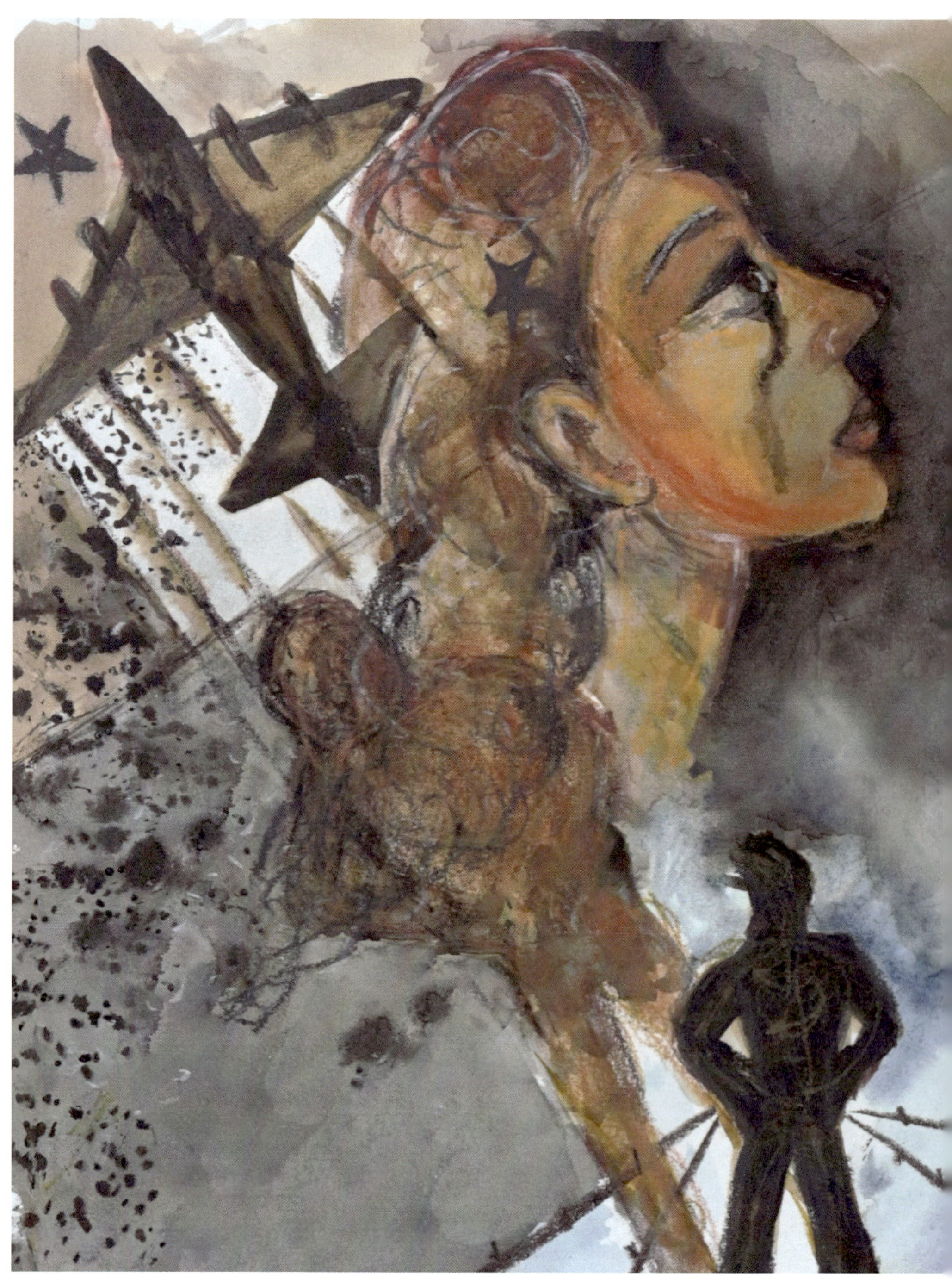

Sister: The Funeral (1)

You say I should have gone to the funeral
since to say goodbye is necessary to mourning.

As if it could have helped to see the military
Guard of Honour enact their ritual validations.

Imagine the salute of sword and gun then think
of his sister who told me he looked 'peaceful'

when she placed my early gifts, a ring, cufflinks
beside him in the coffin, sealing the rites of passion.
I didn't need to see such hopeless internment,
too much, too little already buried.

Sister: The Funeral (2)

At the funeral in my mind
I approach the official widow
wondering what words might lighten
this sisterhood of grief.

When I was with him
                                        inarticulate

between   each   kiss

ignoring   grave   spaces

we could not afford or dare
old four-letter words
time has worn so smooth.

Speech would have been
to   skim   pebbles   across
a   moving   surface
before plunging to darkness.

There is no retrieval
from the depths of loss
between 'love' or 'fuck'
or any cliches of consolation

only this stumbling

            into   metaphor

that will not speak   to him,   to her,

            black figures   haunting.

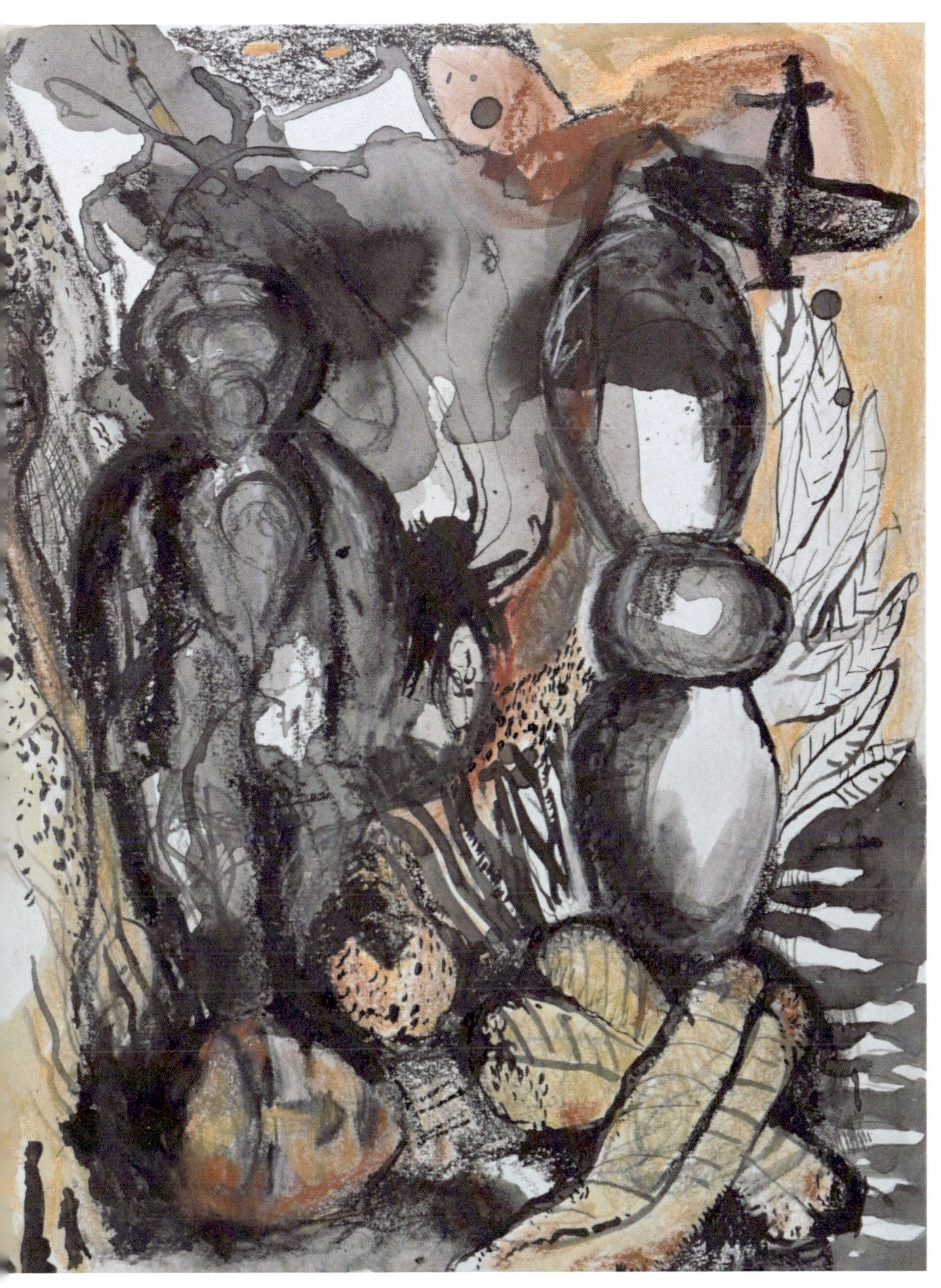

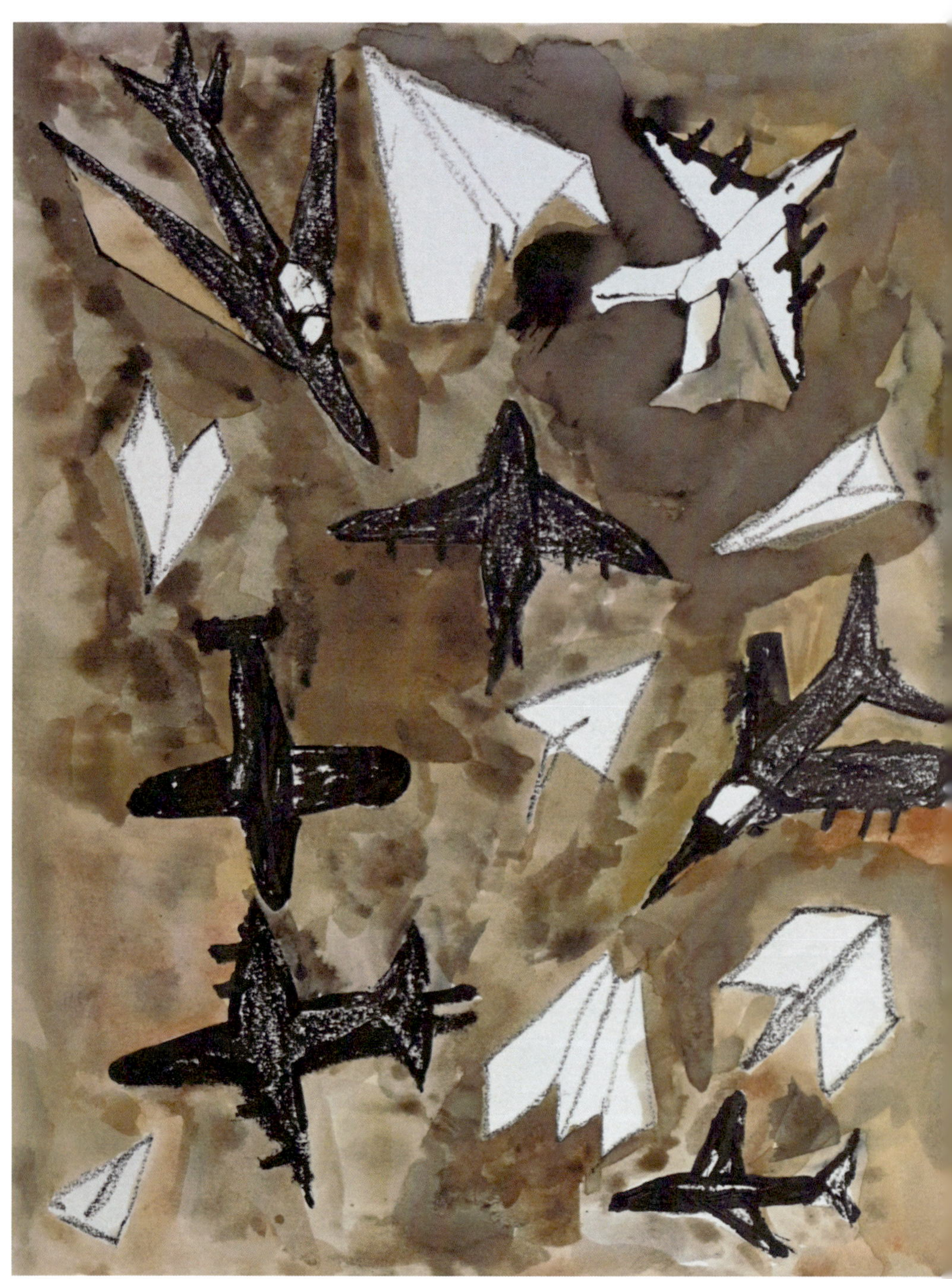

Brother: Martial Art

In the pub we sat together,
I smoked saying, 'I want to write.'

He took a white handkerchief
holding it taut before his face

gestured with a finger I should place
the smoke between his lips.

He took a drag, exhaled
a brown stain spread across the cotton.

'Imagine your lungs,' he said,
'If you want to write, write

spare me the agony.' So, I see him
stride away, strapping on the bone-dome,

an action man harnessing jet power
to cavort from the sky,

off the page, leaving me behind
a last drag, which tastes of ash.

Brother: Fantasy

Look! Me
at the controls
landscape revolves
we are upside down

a jerk of the stick
plane flips over
triumphant roll and waggle
of wings.

Is it simply a display
of spurious skill
this dazzling, heroic performance
for the crowd's applause

or is there more of self-delight
a process of investigation
appraising the limits
of possibility?

I write in imitation
of flight.
See me steer from nothing
to nothing.

Out of trouble
my crash is comic.

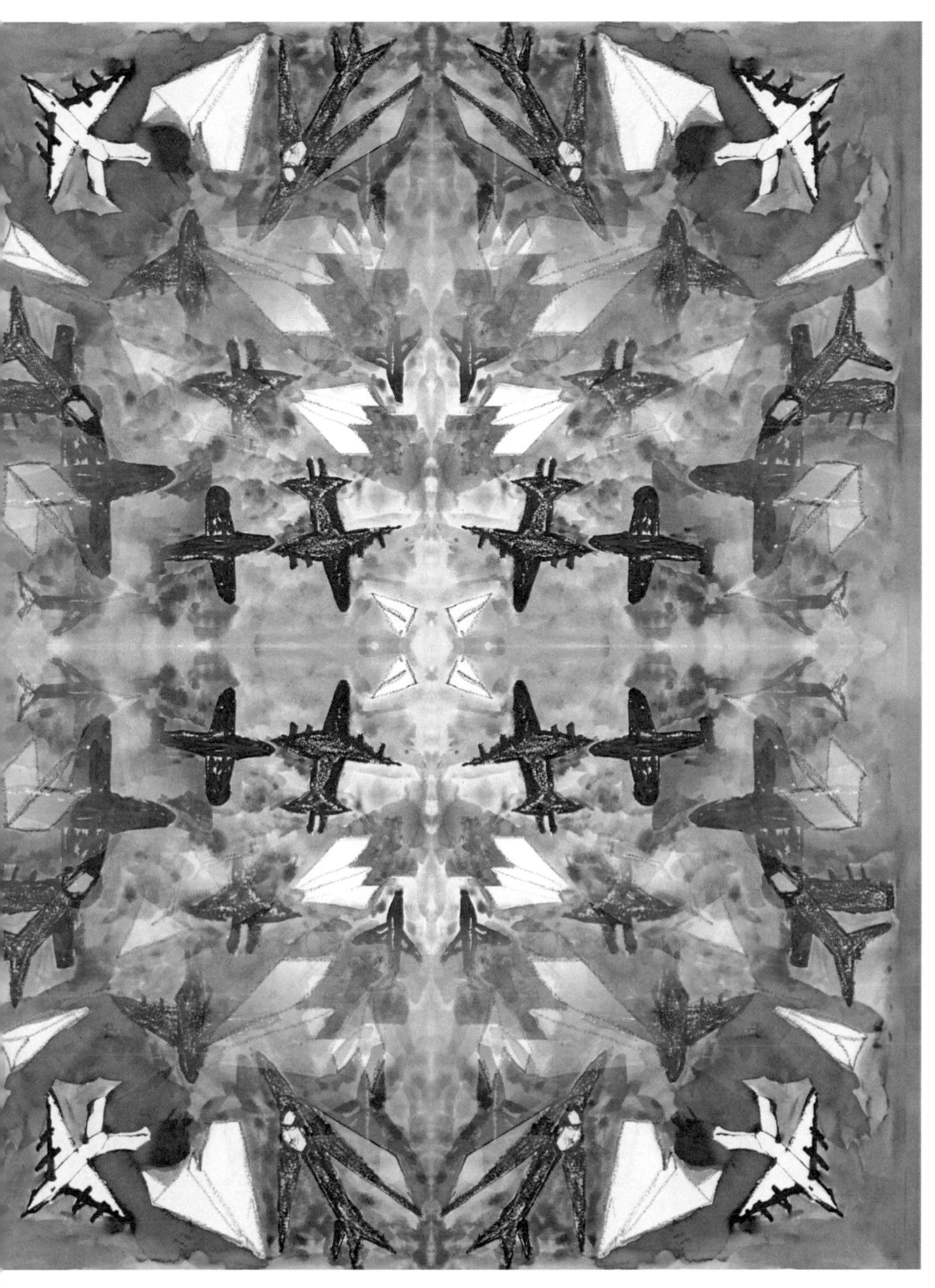

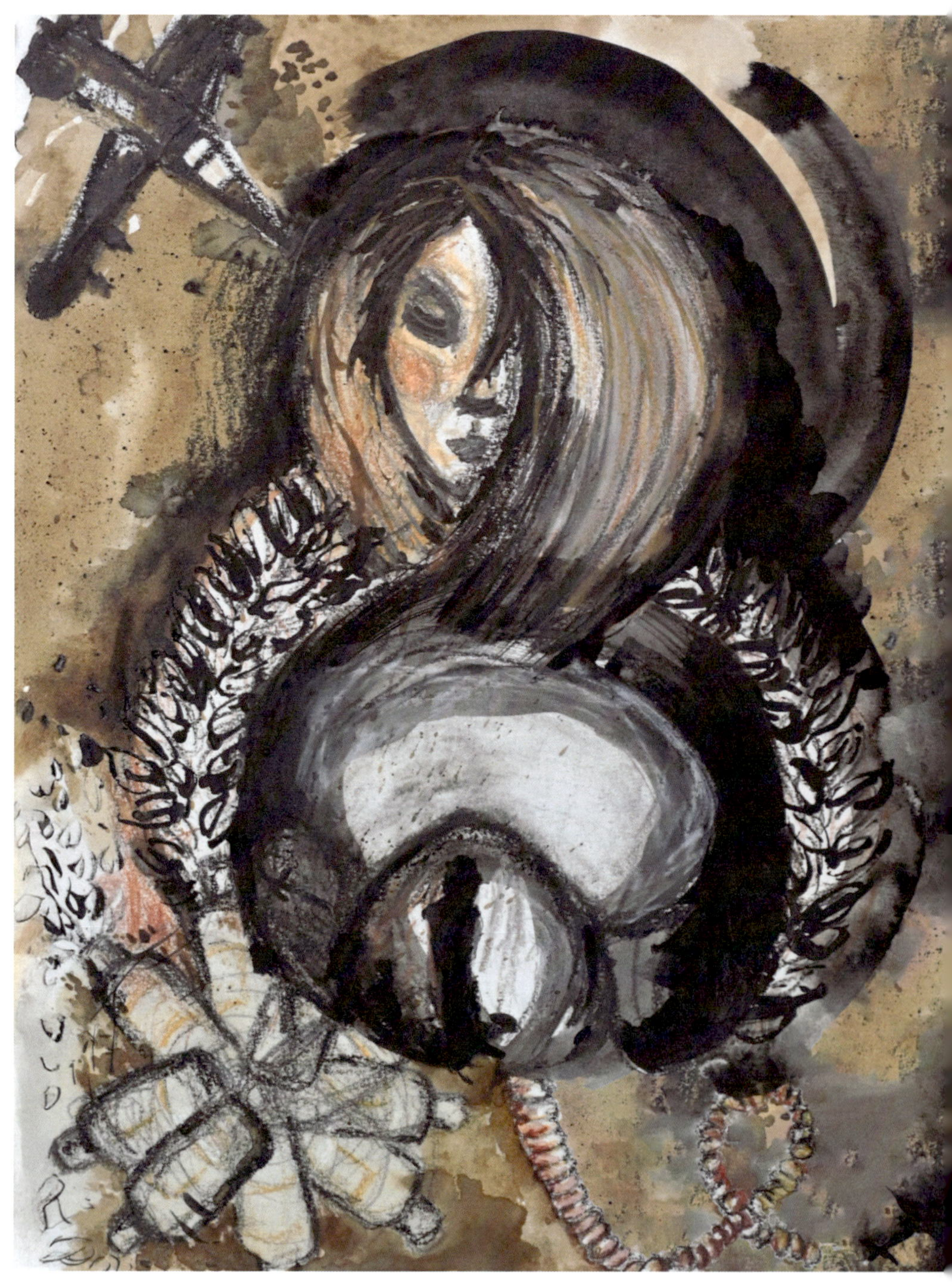

Sister: Re-Write

I want to re-write this story.
It is hard to plainly say,
at thirteen, I met him,
at nineteen, I slept with him.
My parents disapproved
not of my choice but
sex before marriage.
Betrayed by a family friend
they found out. My father
raged, called me a whore.
My mother speaking of love-
making said, *you'll soon*
get tired of him
          messing you about.

Grounded and fearful
I couldn't anymore. He had an affair.
Ours ended. We married the wrong
partners.

          Later through letters
we met again   ignoring spouses
          he parked his G-suit   bone-
dome
in my bedroom   through all
          that jaunty slang
we flew towards   this crash.

          These, then, are the facts.

Brother: His Triumph Spitfire

Children of the early fifties we were brought up
on stories of the war: comic strips and movies
Paddy Payne: Spitfire Pilot, *Reach for*
the Sky, *633 Squadron*, *The Dam Busters*,
and those weepy re-runs of the forties,
The Way to the Stars, *Target for Tonight*;
all those laughing, dashing cavaliers
in blue roaring to the pub
in their open-top sports,
sing-songs round the tired piano,
the doomed encounters with misty-eyed WAAFs
who saw their desperate darlings off to die,
and gave such potent prelude to your story.
I can see him now in the fire red Triumph
outside our house, uniformed in bravado,
primed and ready to join the ranks of the early dead
taking his place in the annals of fatal romance.

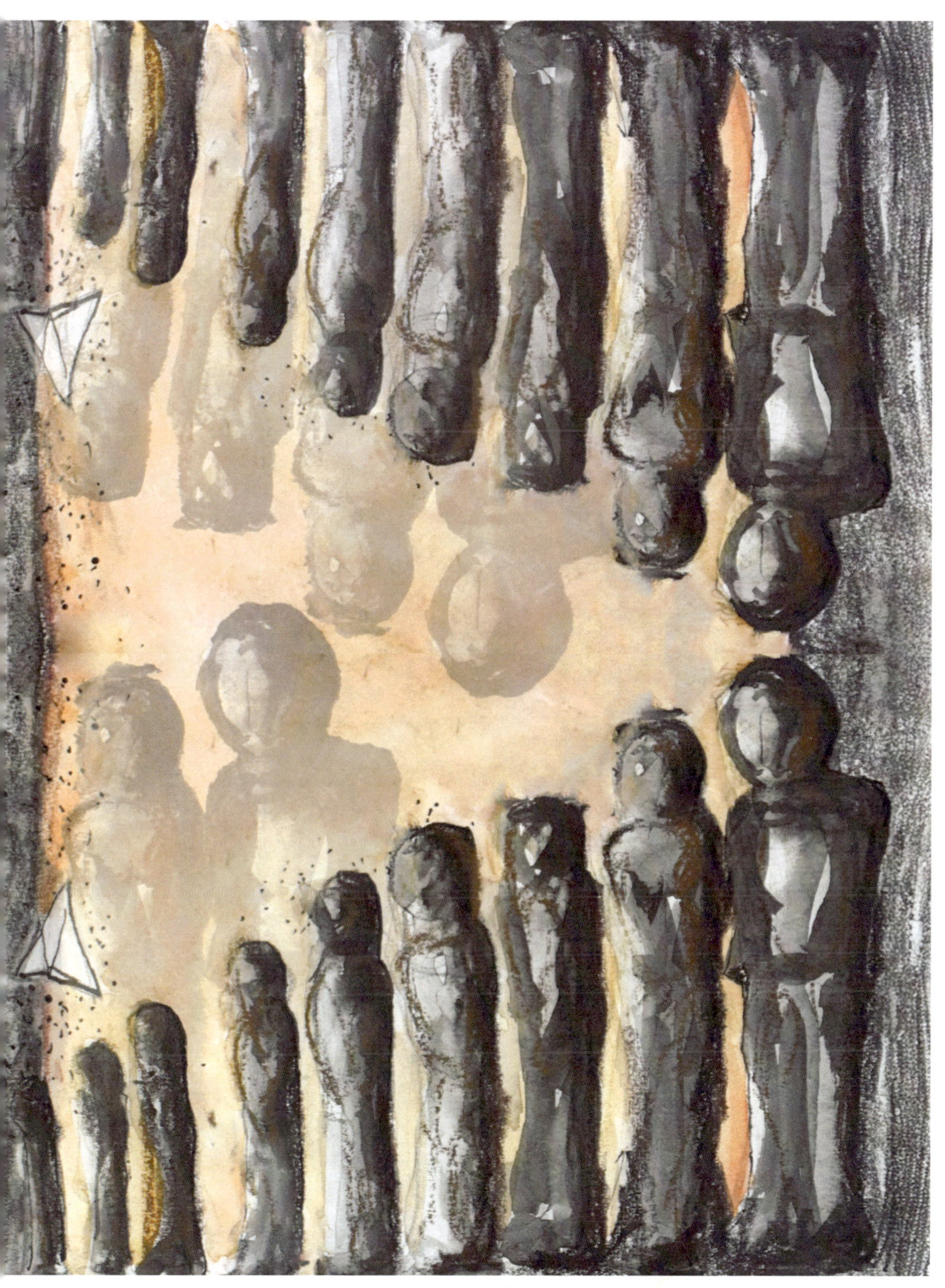

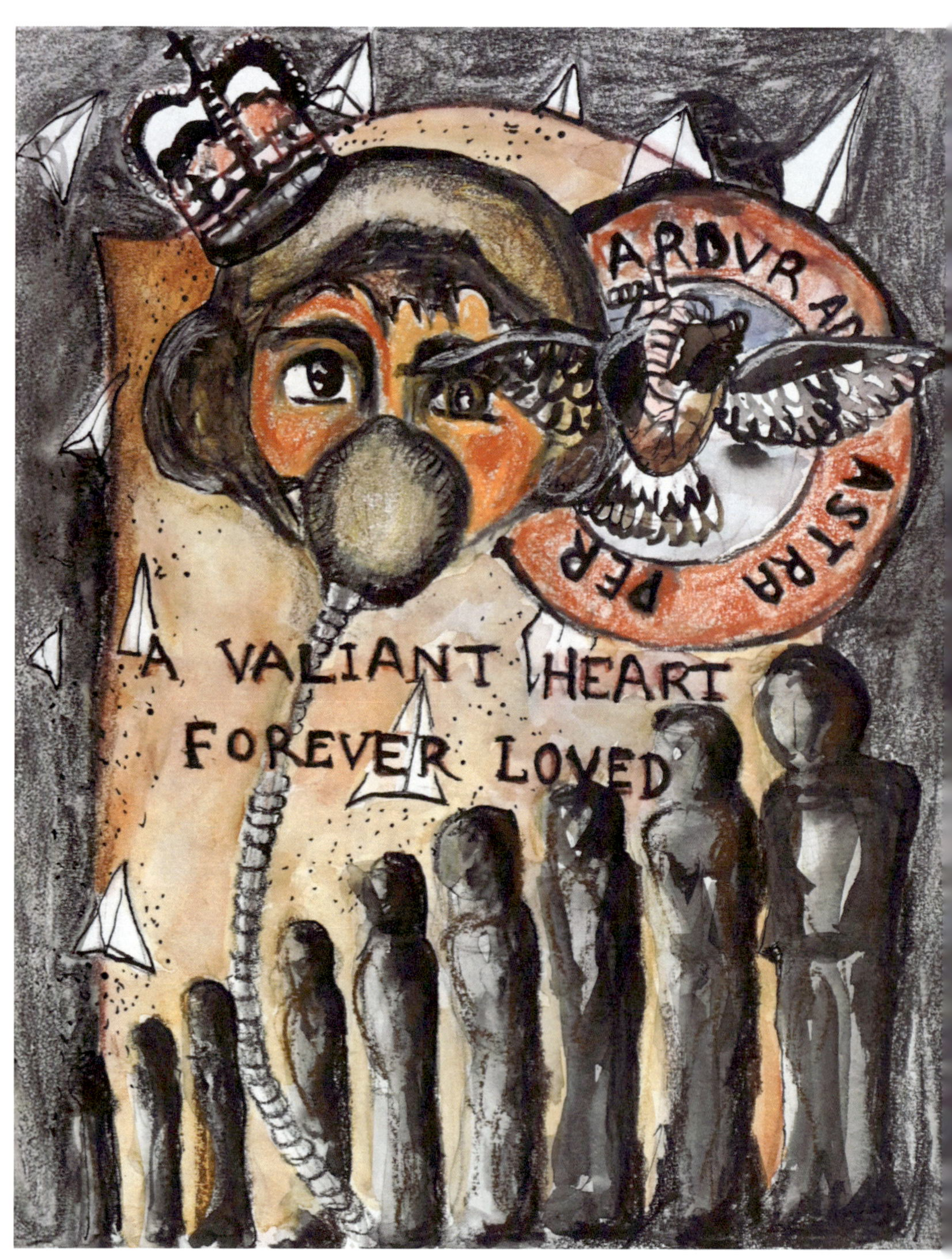
ARDVR A
ASTRA
PER
A VALIANT HEART
FOREVER LOVED

Sister: Doubts about the mission

People thought I was in love
with the uniform.
Never that naïve I used to joke
of his enticement from
Boy Scout to Flight Lieutenant –

all those vows and creeds
a way of clothing chaos
to make things safe.
He'd laugh but rarely speak
of meaning or belief.

If pressed he would murmur

of peace
keeping
forces
of darkness
at bay

rogue eyes the only clue to irony.
You surrender yourself, I'd say,
an absurd leap of faith
in cynical governments.

What if they should ask aggression of you?
Would you launch the dutiful bomb or rocket
raining death from the skies
without question or reason?

His resort would be to literature,
the only poem he knew, I'd taught him:

I only think of flight, he said,
'a lonely impulse of delight'.

Brother: Re-Write

drove

impulse to

lonely this

a tumult

delight in

the

of

clouds

Brother: The Briefing

That word is never used. He points to

the abstract image on a map, the world

made flat. 'The target for

to-night (classified) gentlemen is destruction

of enemy installations, infrastructure, supply. The

weather: cloud base variable, moon, no moon, minor

turbulence can be expected, navigational co-ordinates

follow. Possible anti-aircraft activity, ground to air, sea

to air, air-to-air'. There is no mention of delight, but

plenty of bravado. 'Good-luck.' 'Tally-Ho'. The

upper lips so stiff they might shatter if they

cried. And *that* word remains

unspoken. Shhh.

It detonates with

k my darlings.

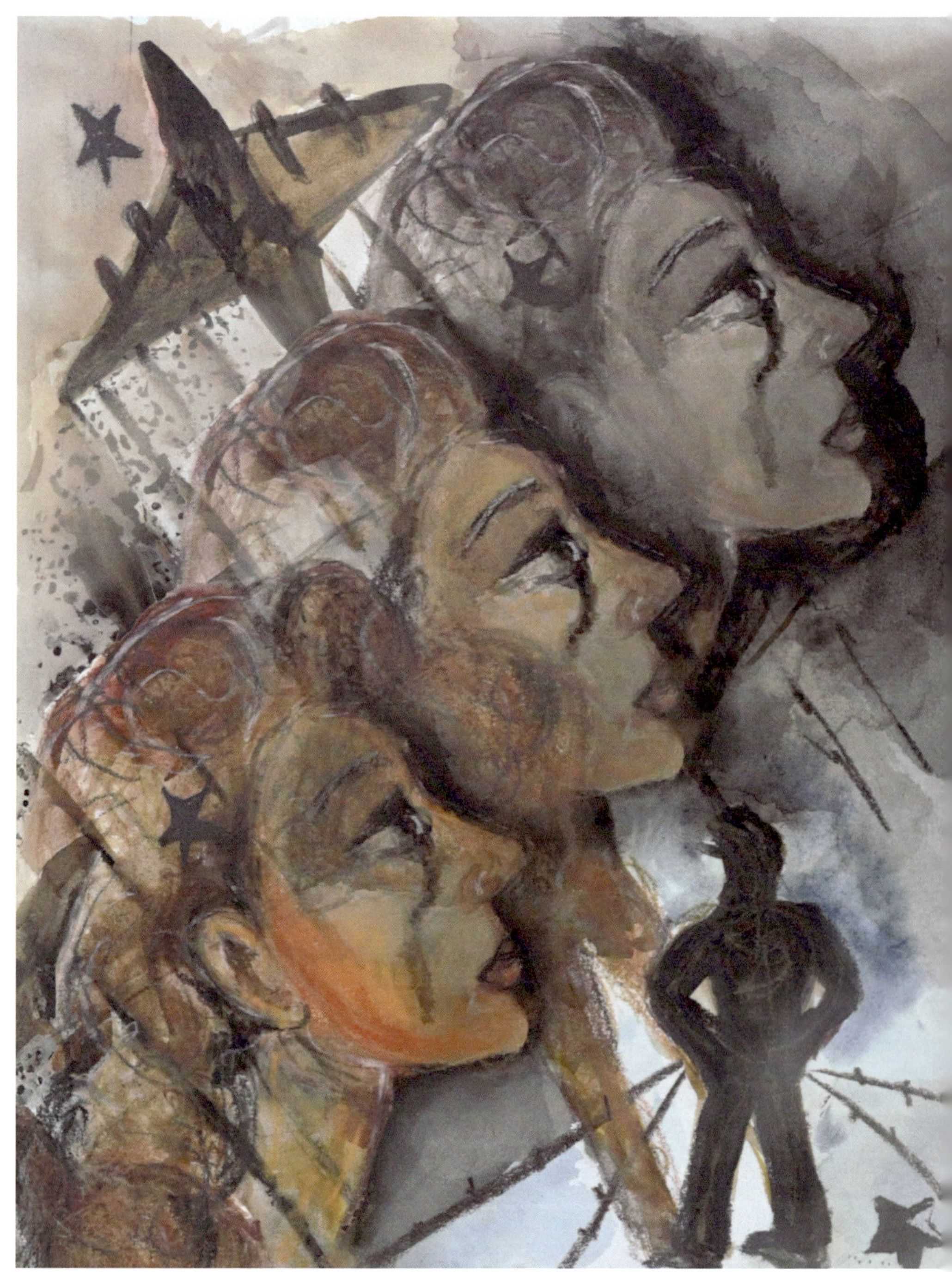

Sister: *Johnny the bright star*

Head-
        In-
                Air
                        Johnny
had no children
                for whom
                        we might care
                                        to explain

how he came to be

                                        the bright star.

All those glittering

                sharp pricks
                                of light

        marble

                fragments

                        on the slab

                                of night

bright

                romantic   fictions.

Bloody Mars
                shines red

                        Venus is sickly green.

What wings we had

                        are broken.

Brother: Sister's Story

Shards of nightmare
cut light
to
strips
horror through
the hands' curtain
drawn at breakfast
she hurls outside
and flings her lover's gift
the trivial treasure
of a coffee mug
against the wall
its colours
crack

suddenly shocking

white slivers

of unglazed clay
litter the grass
defining rage.

Petrified,
eyes closed, she pictures
the silent wreckage
runs towards
the shattered canopy
which reveals his staring eyes
last seen
glazed
with desire.
Now she glances
sees white
the splintered
bone
and so returns
to her morning garden
where she weeps and kneels
to gather the
pieces.

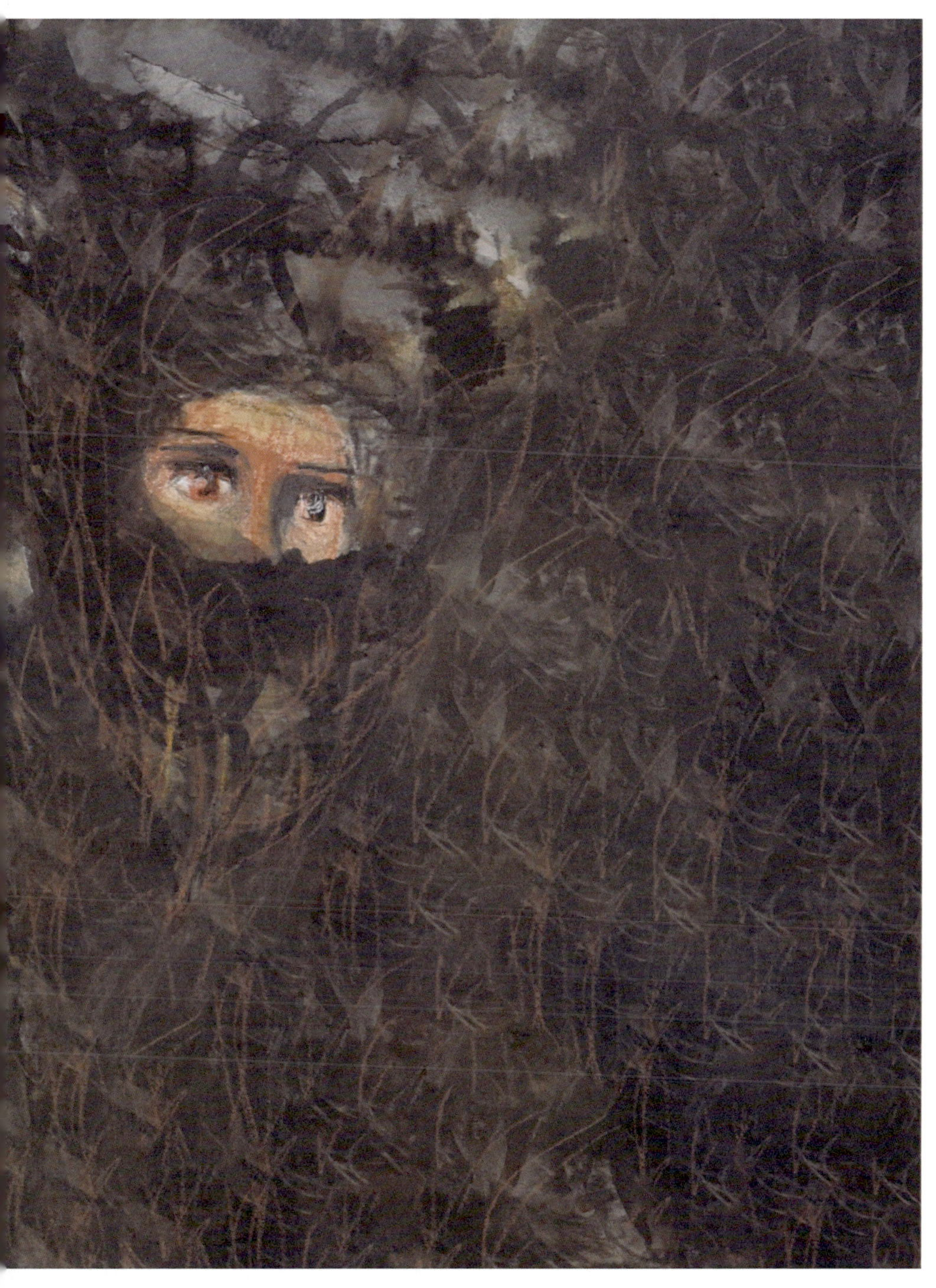

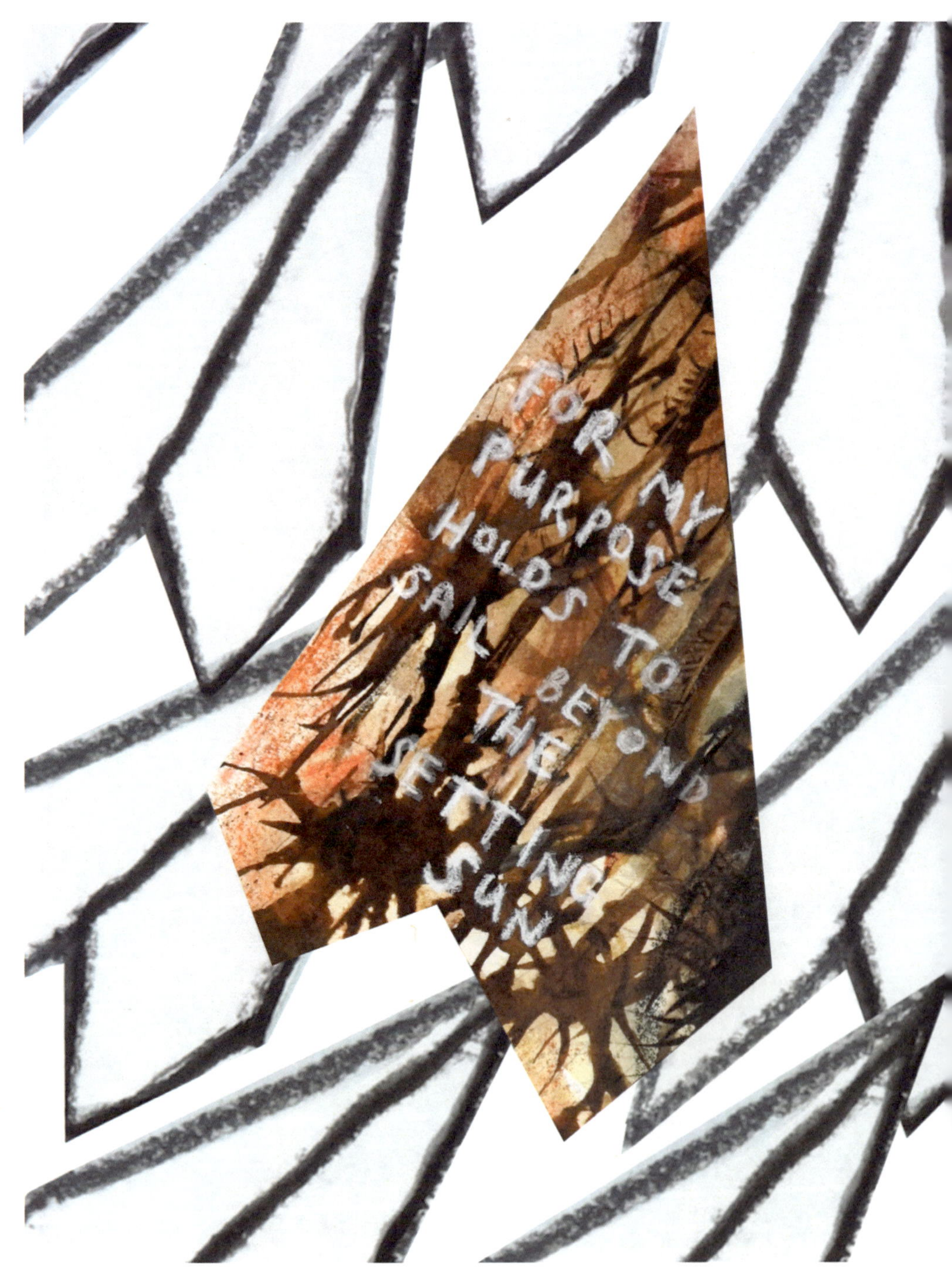
FOR MY
PURPOSE
HOLDS TO
SAIL BEYOND
THE
SETTING
SUN

Brother: Ways of Seeing, Ways of Being

He could not bear   a desk job
        wife   two kids   suburban villa
half-conversations   every night
                                a slow dribble of spirit
weekends   lawn-mowing   only escape   the car-wash
                        all to play for
ascending wealth
                        consuming   passion.

No contest flight's excitement – the Jaguar – Mach I
over NATO borders   how he would describe it –
low-level
        beneath
                the radar
        intercepting opposing aircraft
                you   machine   target
        concentration absolute
                                to be distracted
is to   die.

Afterwards   beers in the mess   celebratory
        every day   you play the biggest game,
                        flying from boredom,   domestic routine
        to make   the world your own
risking   the anarchic moment   alone,

head in the clouds

                I want to say like mine
                                    as I write
                but my adventure is all

in mind   the hazard

smaller.

Sister: Per Ardua Ad Astra

wings
angel's
on

up

him

bear

that

bright

and

laughing

boy

the

young

man

playing

a

romantic

lead

uniformed in

the

crimson
sports
car

Icarus

wings the
angel's gently to thrill
on against lost of
up the years speed
him fast the and
Bear fall all power

the

triumph

of

imagination's

dark

seductions

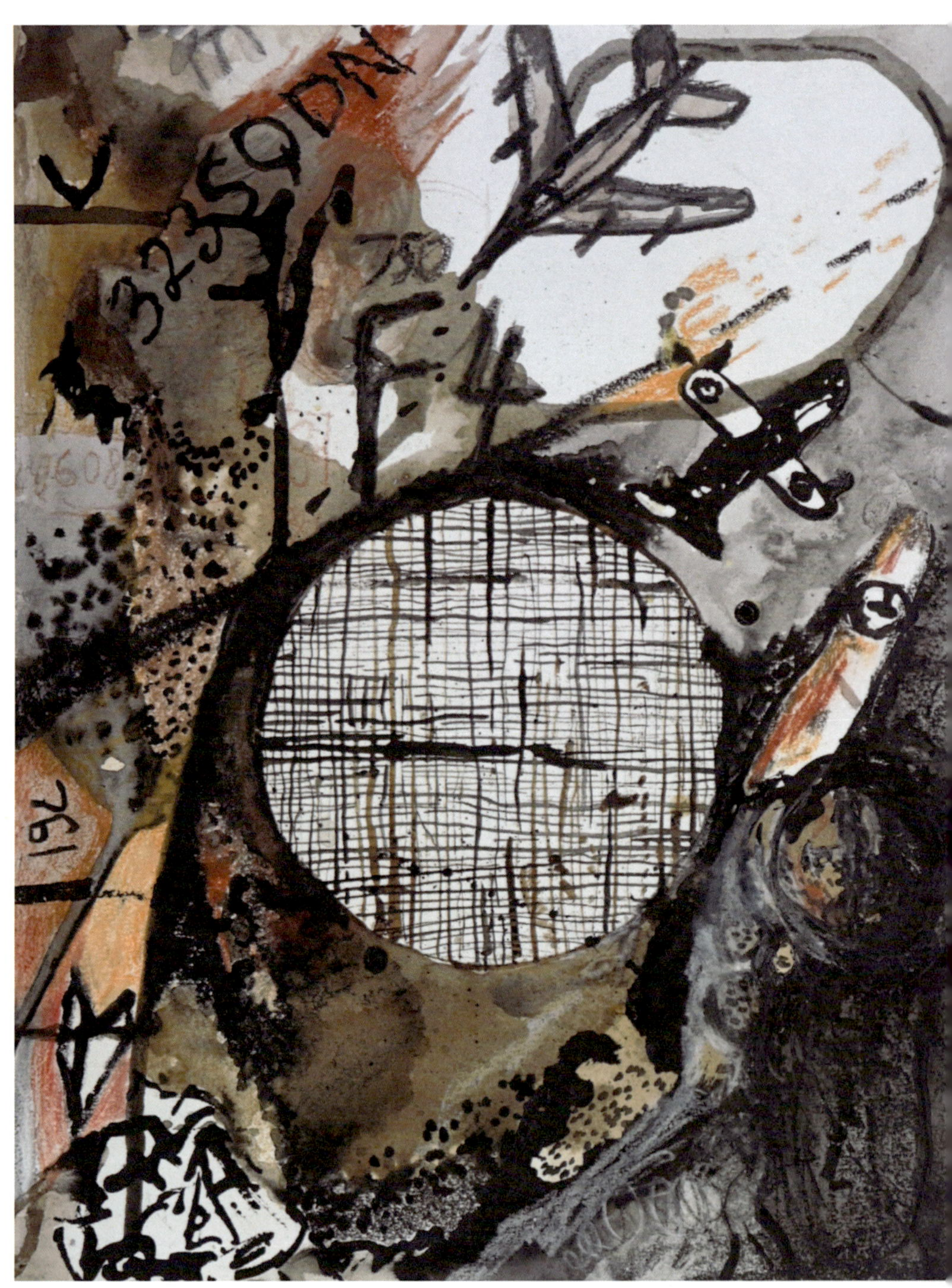
323SQDN
F4

Brother: Documentary

Posted from ops to instructor
selected to represent
his squadron in aerobatics competition.
His CO: 'One of the best pilots
I've ever seen.' Practising
low level, serious games,
a barrel roll goes wrong.
Nobody will ever know why
he mishandled the controls.
He'd flown the sequence twice
that morning with no problems . . .
a tragic accident.

Sister: Reminisces

You will remember our gaudy night
before you left for Australia
how bright and drunk we were

over the brandy in the
interstices of grief and laughter
how I told you

he'd been visiting, the illicit affair,
and how he'd said that only I
could be the mother of his child.

I didn't ask about his wife,
I didn't need to; what was there
more to say after this remark?

I don't know how the story
would have ended. There
are tears enough for a lifetime

in this abrupt full-stop.

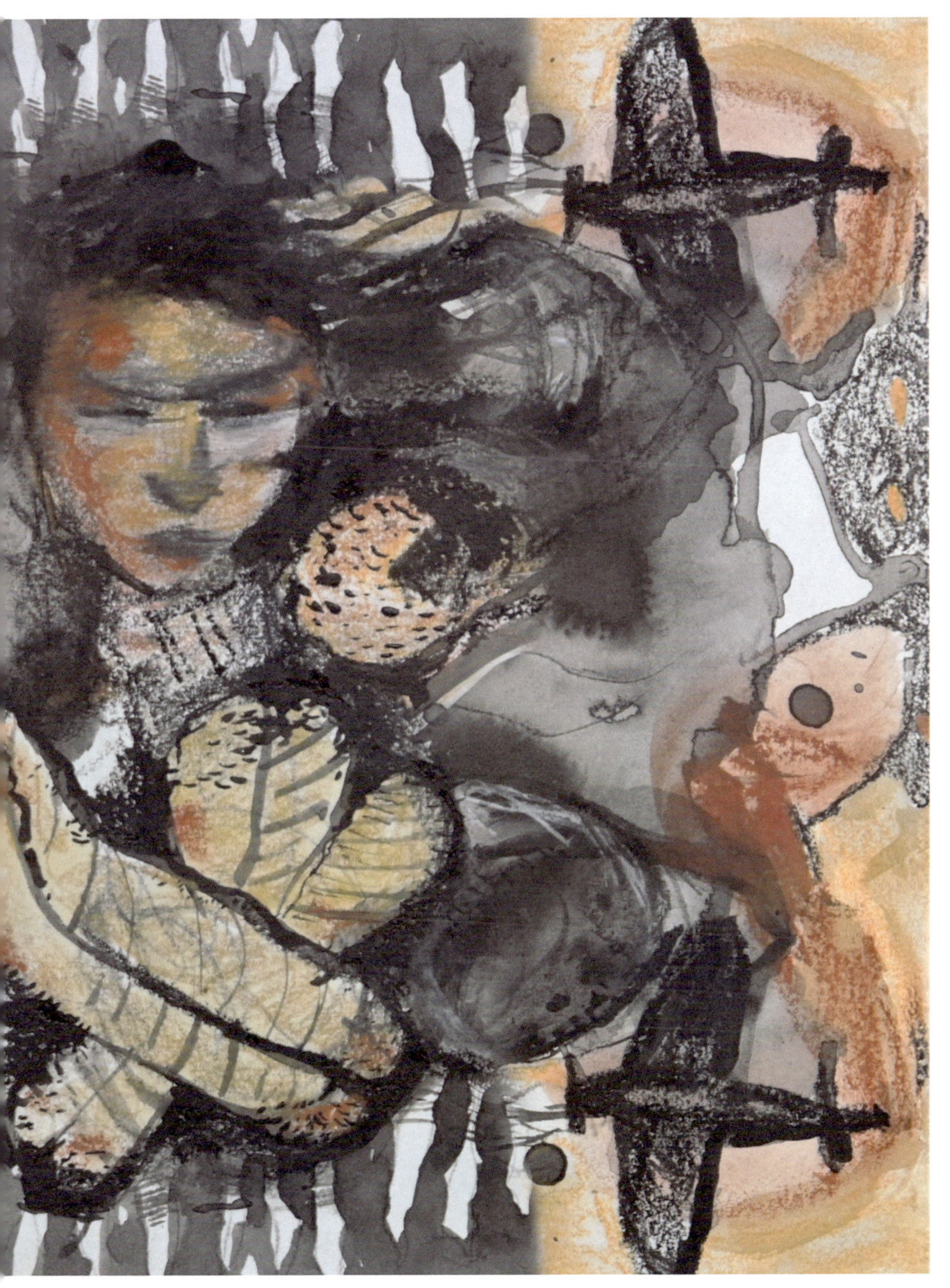

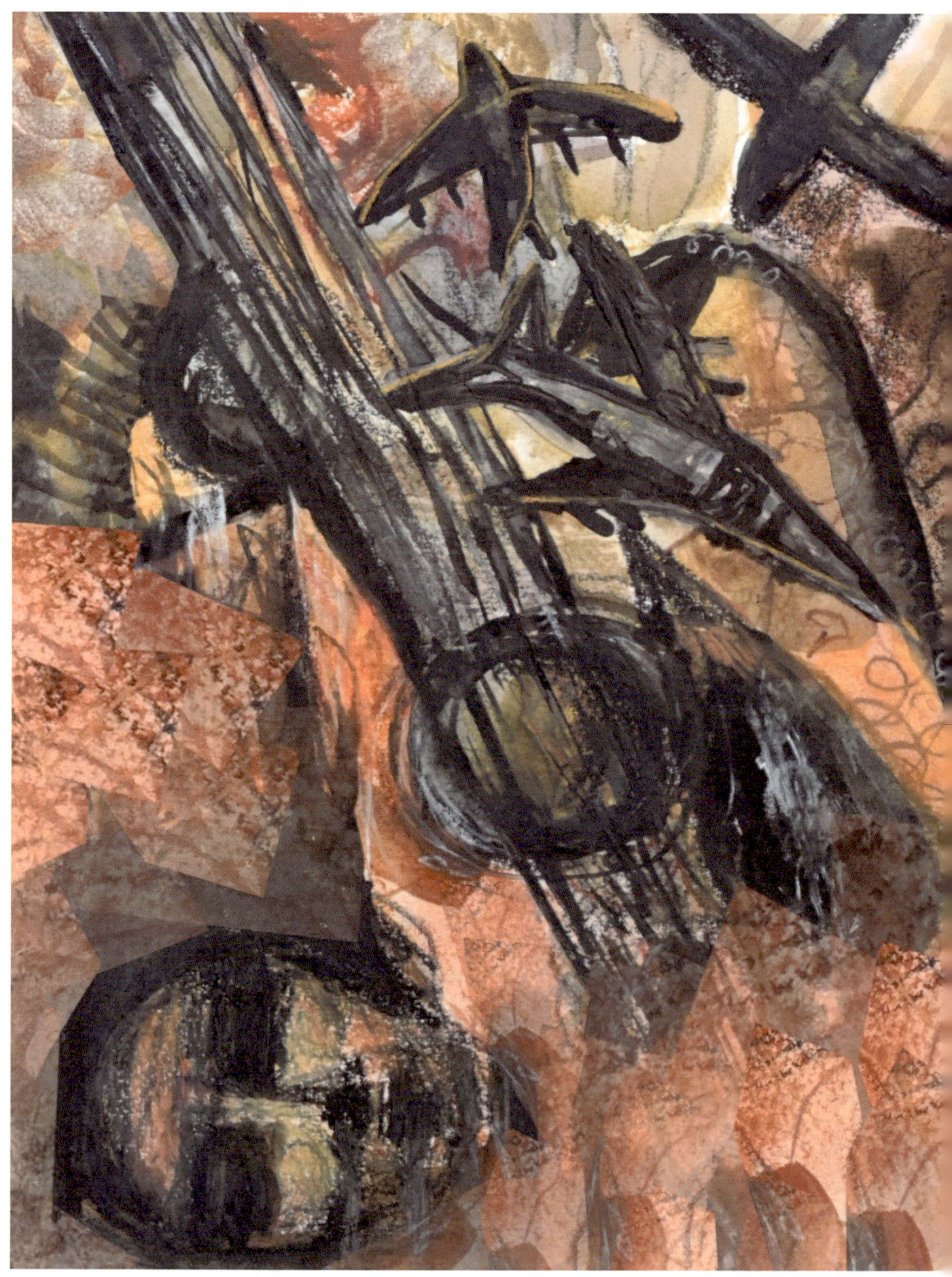

Brother: *Soldier, Scholar, Horseman, he*

He was the bright and laughing boy,
adept at games, witty, clever,
with the cheeky grin and charming banter,
two years ahead of me at school
he had the confident dash I always craved,
my sister's love for him measured all my lack
and when he joined the RAF, pilot training,
how small I always felt beside him.
My only defence this troubadour pose –
my mournful songs and strumming,
no compensation for his endless flight.

Sister: On Continuing

From my window
        bird flies
with no apology
        some die

flying into obstacles
        they can't see
so investigation falters
        understanding only
a manufacture of excuses.

Should I just say
        we were impelled
to break in different ways
        elderly codes
of behaviour
        flying blind
into disastrous freedom

a passionate venture to be
        only to end
hitting a pane
        of glass
as the small bird dead
        among the stones.

Reflective   look
        how the mate hops
bereft   until hopeless
        flies again.

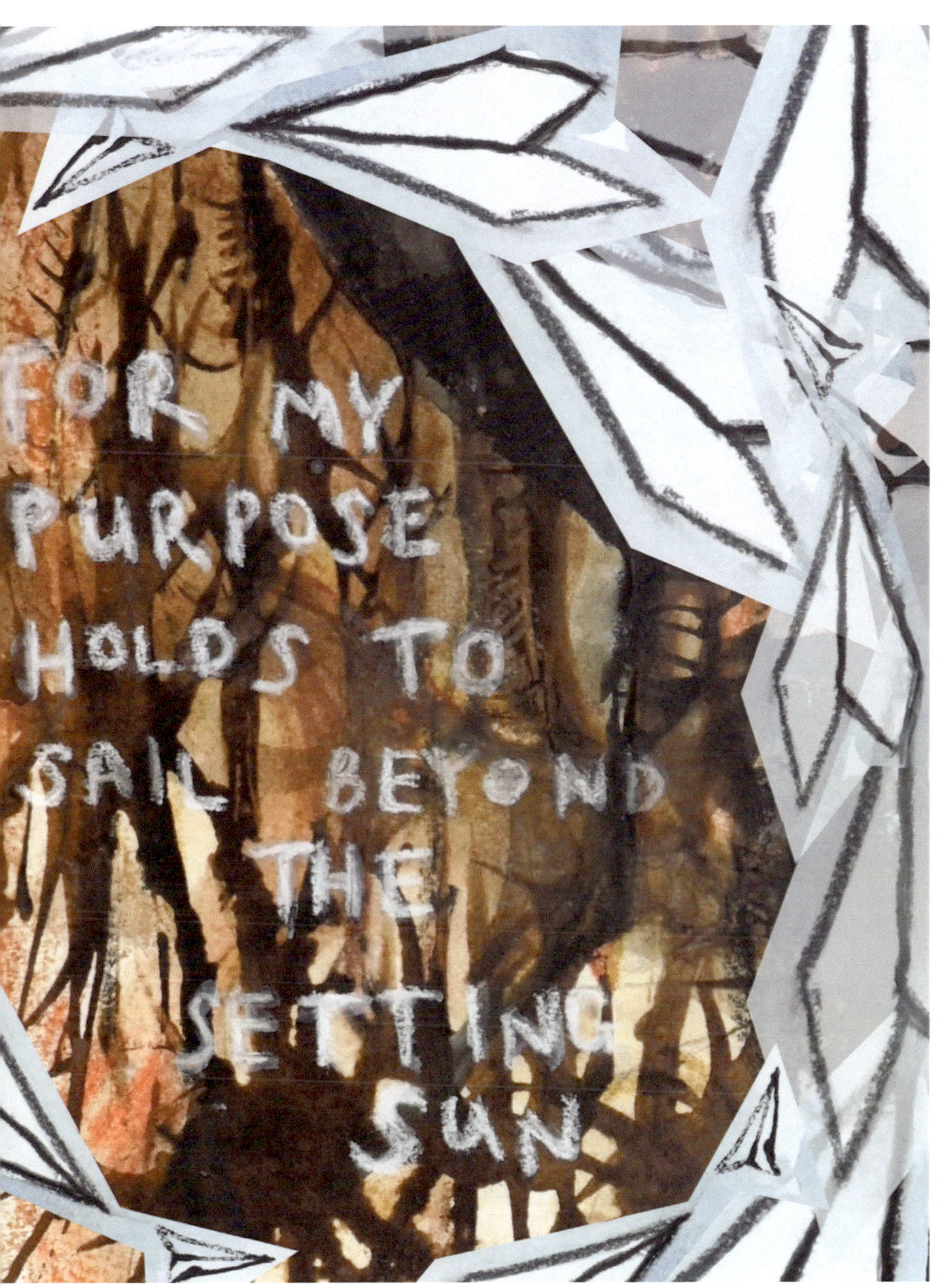
FOR MY
PURPOSE
HOLDS TO
SAIL BEYOND
THE
SETTING
SUN

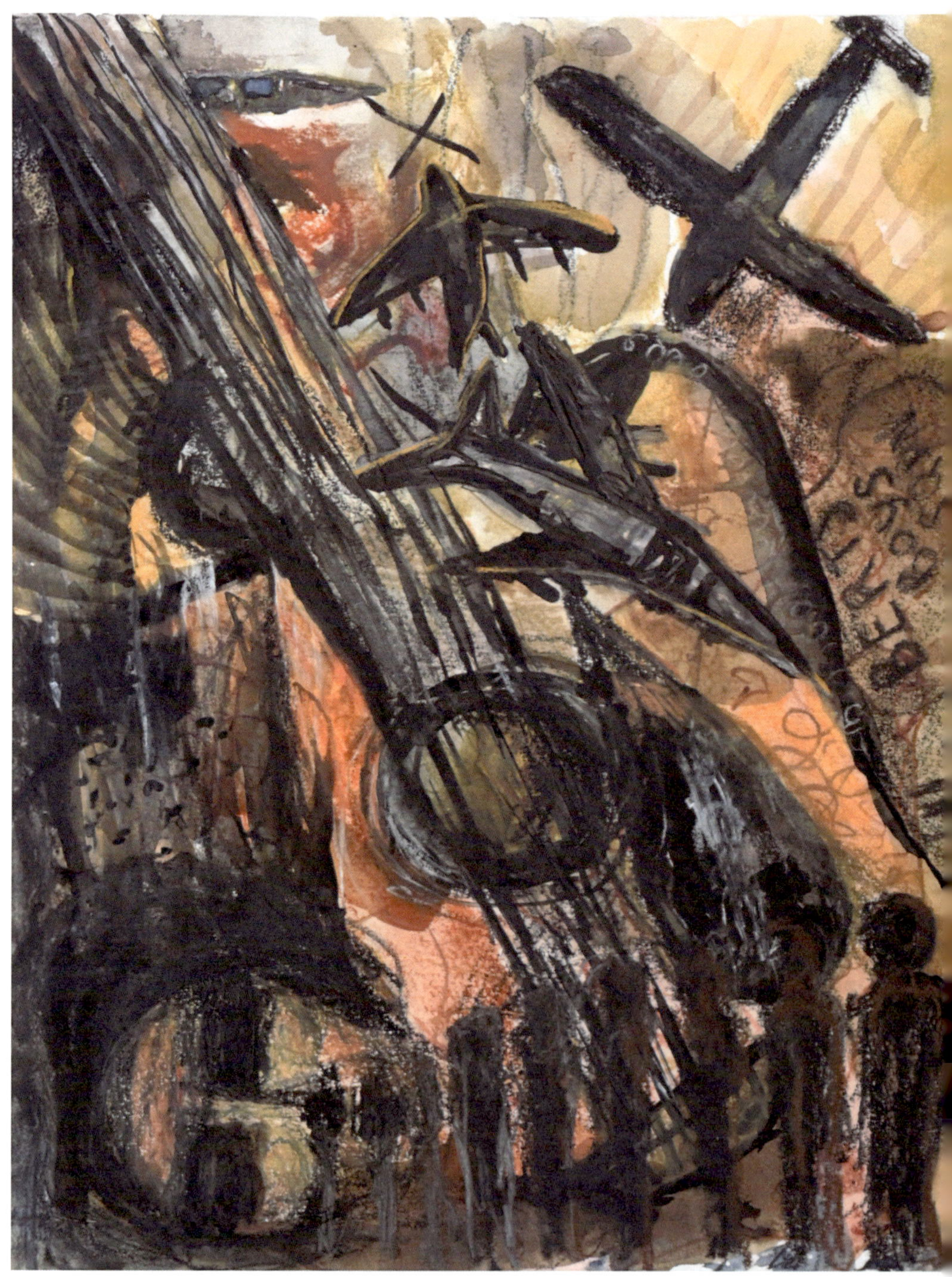

Brother and Sister: The Eagle

Those years in Cambridge, it was always the Eagle

for lunch, my sister was quick the first time

to show me the reason we were there

in the back room pointing to

the ceiling inscribed with signatures

of flight crew who used the pub

for obvious reasons in World War II.

'Imagine those boys,' she said,

'just learning to be men, on the table, climbing

drunk on each other's shoulders

to reach and scribe their mark – the delusion of

a smoke stained

immortality

Johnny, Geoff, Will and Rob were here but now

are gone.

I don't need to tell you how it makes me feel,

the ghosts of all those doomed

pilots, navigators, gunners, bomb aimers,

their awful legacy of

strange and hopeless glamour.'

Brother: Leavings

On the windowsill in your spare room
where I stayed visiting from Australia,
a copy of *Enduring Love*, a novel
scalpel bright with sinister possibilities.

Protruding from the cover, as if a bookmark,
a card from his sister to thank-you
for the May-time flowers you sent
in remembrance every year.

The novel begins with an aerial accident, a death.
There are mistaken ideas about an illicit affair.
There is religious obsession and deranged violence.
There is the collision of partners –

one devoted to science and reason, the other
an expert on Keats, attuned to emotion, intuition
empathy. I thought of your pilot lover
and your English studies, your fondness for

Keats and Yeats, his Physics degree, and how,
perhaps you were in the process of reconciling
differences, before he died. In his flight
beyond reason he left you with nothing

but the consolations of sentiment,
sisterly sharing of anniversaries,
an everlasting exchange between
bent steel and withered blooms.

The glacial novel leaves no room for
nostalgic memories of love gone wrong,
emotion subject to knife's niggle and
probe, consolation of cold minds.

I never spoke to you about the book or marker.
In the novel the dead man is a plot device.
Some like their art served cold
to avoid the stories no one can explain.

I think again of those last cockpit
moments, the barrel roll gone wrong,
the attempt to eject too late, a few seconds
knowledge before oblivion.

Now you've also gone into the dark,
I'm left with what endures. His gift of rings
you gave me for my grand-girls,
And a story, art, these poor remains.

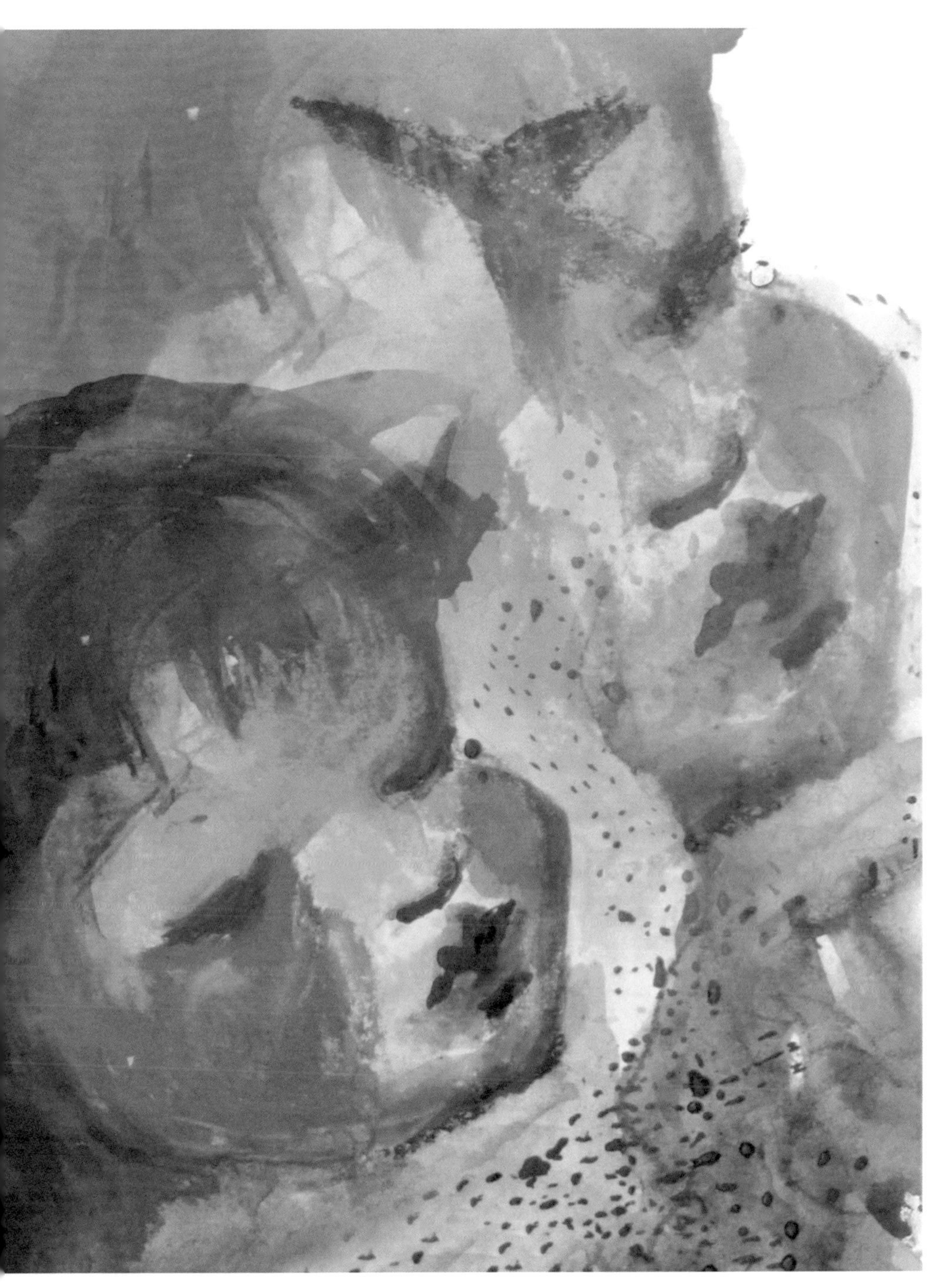

Brother: In the Churchyard

I

After your death, no resolution:
I'm suddenly seeing you
standing by his grave,

a trip I know you made
from home to Linton-on-Ouse
that feted aerodrome,

the tarmac and buildings replete
with the ghosts of all those lost
young men of Bomber Command,

their sweethearts mouthing sorrow
to the empty skies, as they search
for heroes unreturning.

You joined their ranks
after your lover's needless
death   his only fight

against himself, the falling
fatal plunge to earth,
all wings sheared.

II

Did you go to All Saints in autumn
through damp grass and rotting
leaves, or in ironic

spring, the early flowers,
snowdrop and daffodil,
nodding by the granite

stone of service, badged
with eagle, cross and motto,
Per Ardua ad Astra,

*A Valiant Heart Forever
Loved*, the words rising
to the remembrance tune.

Did it echo through your
skull, so many brass bands,
so many choirs around

the village cross mouthing
the lies of that seductive hymn,
the obscene made sacred,

the chivalric knights laying
down their lives in *lesser
calvaries* for God?

III

O Valiant Hearts.
I sang it myself
in the old Church at Frodsham

and at the cenotaph
when we were young,
beguiled by the idea

of our father's, our grandfathers'
exploits. Were you
uplifted there again,

or did you feel the force
of waste, a brutal absence,
the crushing weight of loss?

IV

And as your eyes traversed
the monument, I know
you would translate the Latin

chiselled at the base,
my mind holds course to sail
beyond the setting sun,

Tennyson, turned back,
making your beloved
a Ulysses of the skies,

a desperate stretch
to keep the old ideas
Classics and Christian

alive, in doubtful marriage,
though the hero you loved
didn't return and what we're left

is stone replete with cross
and sword, an apt design
to cover the killing truth.

Notes

Some of the poems in this sequence lean heavily on texts my sister read, some of which she loved. W.B. Yeats's, 'An Irish Airman Foresees his Death,' and John Pudney's poem, 'For Johnny', ('Do not despair/ For Johnny Head-in-Air') which also features in the 1945 film *The Way to the Stars*, are particularly seminal. I also allude to Yeats's poem, 'In Memory of Major Robert Gregory'. In poem IV of 'In the Churchyard' I have offered a translation of the Latin on the headstone, which I imagine my sister might have made. It is a version of the lines from Tennyson's poem *Ulysses* which reads, 'for my purpose holds/to sail beyond the sunset.' Ian McEwan's novel, *Enduring Love*, (Johnathan Cape, 1997) plays a large role in my poem, 'What Remains'. Lastly, for those too young to remember, a Triumph Spitfire was a small, convertible sports car. It was made between 1962 and 1980.

About the Author

Adrian Caesar was born near Manchester in the UK but has lived and worked in Australia for over forty years. He was formerly Associate Professor of English at UNSW@Canberra and subsequently taught creative writing on an occasional basis at ANU. He is the author of fourteen books including fiction, non-fiction and poetry. His experimental non-fiction novel, *The White*, won the Victorian Premier's Award for non-fiction and the ACT Book of the Year in 2000. His poems have been long and short-listed for various awards including the Judith Wright Prize, the Dorothy Porter Prize and the Canberra International Poetry Prize.

About the Artist

Kat Rae is a multidisciplinary artist living in Naarm (Melbourne). Her practice is shaped by 20 years of service in the Australian Army. In 2000, her first year of service, Kat met Adrian, who taught her literature at the Australian Defence Force Academy. Kat's work often draws on personal experience, including the loss of her veteran husband to suicide in 2017 – a turning point that led her to pursue her passion for art. In 2024, Kat graduated with First Class Honours from RMIT's School of Art, where she was awarded the Social Change Prize. That same year, she won the Australian War Memorial's prestigious Napier Waller Art Prize. Kat exhibits regularly and her works are held in the collections of the Australian War Memorial, the Shrine of Remembrance, and the Australian National Veterans Art Museum.

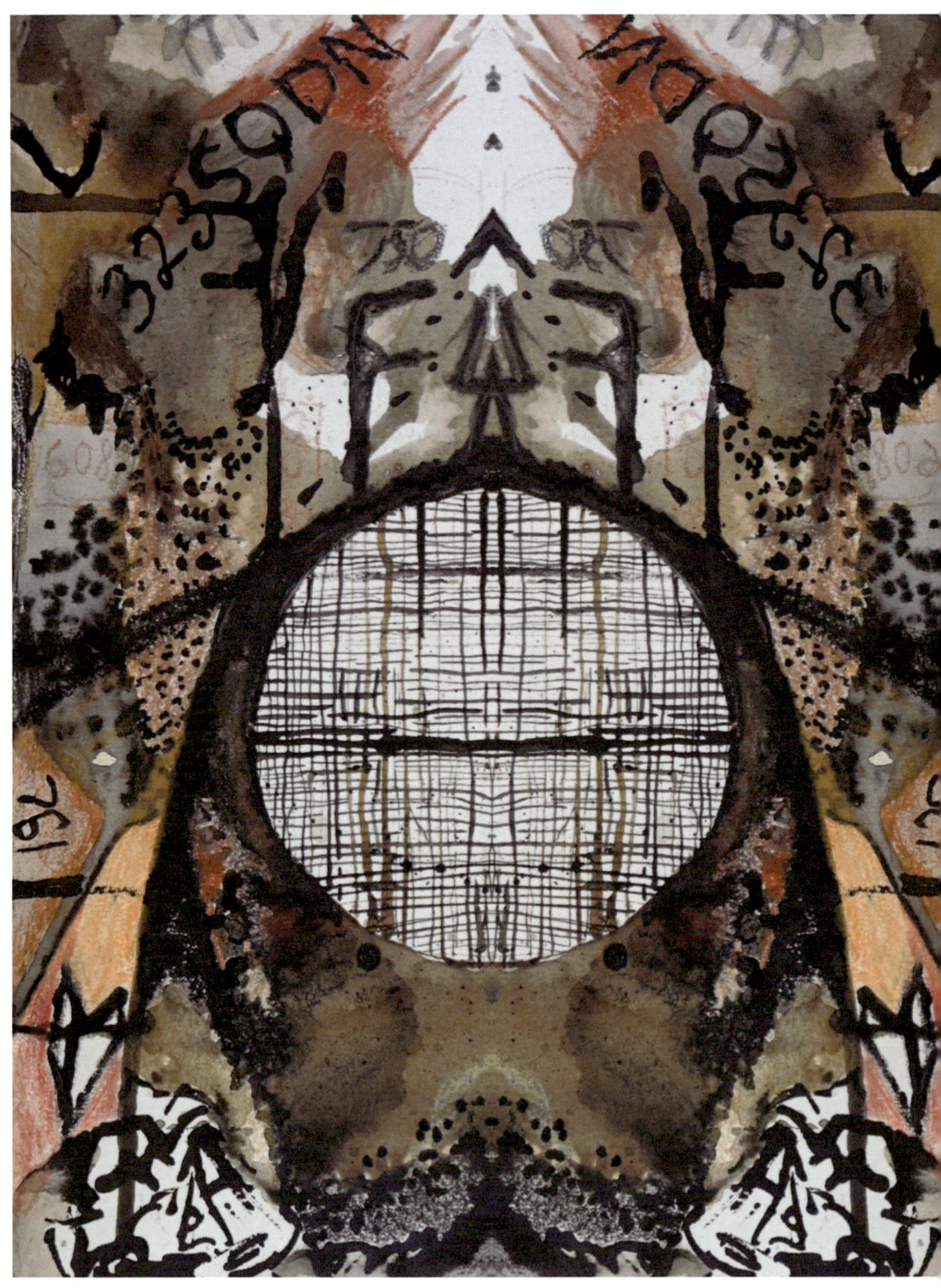

Epilogue

Brother: Flight of Fancy

When you were young before it all went wrong
your dashing RAF cadet would call
driving his fire-red Triumph Spitfire,
to whisk you off to the Station ball.
On training flights, he'd buzz our house
salute with dipping wings and soar.

And then he died, your beloved man,
practising aerobatics in a cloudy May –
a high-speed low-level accident
all those years ago and you were left
forever with what might have been
and sentimental views of uniforms.

My second time at your graveside
It seemed too pat like some bad movie-scene
alone and wanting only to talk with you
when I heard the single-engine plane
over Barton Glebe. I saw the pilot
loop then flatten and flip a victory roll.

For a moment I thought the revenant
was reassuring me, not favouring you
with his display, as if to answer 'yes'
to a query I wish I'd made but refrained
worried it might seem too personal
or betray a mind knocked daft with sorrow.

As you were dying, I wanted to ask
if you found some comfort in the thought
of joining your first great love in some
fast beyond, *the lonely impulse of dolight*
redeemed; the broken pact made whole:
imagination's lovely recompense.

Cavorting above the burial ground,
inscribing vapour trails across the blue,
the pilot left an airy scribble
fading like invisible ink – a child's trick
or adult conceit to make a secret sign:
the plane rolled again, then flew out of sight.

I'm left with absence and the mystery
of an imperfect metaphor for why I write:
the wish these airy trails of rhetoric
spun in a paroxysm of self-delight
could conjure you in an indelible salute;
the ink permanent, the magic absolute.

Acknowledgements

Kat and Adrian would like to acknowledge the Traditional Owners of the stolen land on which they make and write: the people of the eastern Kulin nations the Boon Warring and Woi Warring and those of the Walbunja of the Yuin nation. We pay our respects to their Elders past and present.

We would also like to thank the following friends and colleagues for their wonderful work in helping to bring this project to fruition: Vani Newby, a print-based artist of Naarm (Melbourne), who collaborated with Kat to reinterpret and expand her Sky Writing sequence through digital collage; Soile Paloheimo, print-based artist and graphic designer, who designed and typeset the book, (Palo Design Ltd); and, Shane Strange for agreeing to put the finishing touches to the production and publish the work.

www.ingramcontent.com/pod-product-compliance
Ingram Content Group Australia Pty Ltd
76 Discovery Rd, Dandenong South VIC 3175, AU
AURC010146090726
429626AU00001B/1

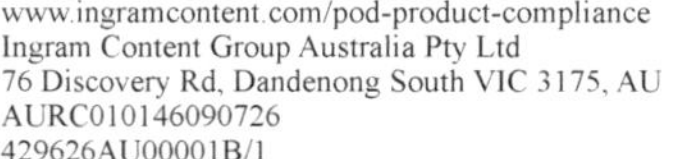

* 9 7 8 1 7 6 4 1 0 6 8 4 9 *

9 781764 106849